For Lucas,

Thank You,
Your Stubby

Copyright © 2021 Stephanie Webb
All rights reserved. No part of this publication may be reproduced, stored in a retrieval system, or transmitted in any form or by any means, electronic, mechanical, recording or otherwise, without the prior written permission of the author.

Printed in the United States of America.

LUCAS, SERVICE DOG

Written and Illustrated by
Ms. Stubby Webb

Author Note:

This book is about my dog, Lucas, and myself. The terms being used are from the year 2021. These terms may change in the future, or mean something completely different. For that reason, I will include a glossary in the back.

If after my time on earth is past, and this book is still being presented, I hope that the future printings will change the terms to match the science and terminology of that present day. I simply ask you add a note to this section to update the year, and include in the glossary the updated terms along with the old terms.

Lucas is a very special dog. He was born April 7, 2020, during the covid pandemic. His service has helped me be able to do things now that I wouldn't be able to do without him. He is truly my best friend and what I also consider the best co-worker one can have.

The drawings in this book are my own. I simply used a mechanical pencil to illustrate. I hope they are as enjoyable to view as it was enjoyable to draw them.

Disabilities are a common issue for many people. For some people, they are terrifying; for others, it can be a challenge to overcome. No matter how you face your disability, you are worthy of respect, love, and encouragement. I hope this book brings you hope. I have done my best not to mention any "triggers" about my past. This is my best way of showing the readers my respect for your own trauma you may have or be having.

I will include information to hotlines and websites of this era (please update for future printings) of places to seek help if you are in crisis or ready to receive help. It does get better. Sometimes it feels like forever, but it does get better.

Best Wishes,
Ms. Stubby and Lucas

My name is Lucas. I am a border collie. I am also a service dog. This is my human. My job is to help my human deal with her PTSD and help her get things when her body is too sore to move due to her having fibromyalgia.

Fibromyalgia is a disorder of nerve and soft tissue. Sometimes my human can't move at all from the pain she feels. She cries sometimes because it hurts so bad. She is a super tough human though. She can take a lot of pain. But some days, it gets too much. So I snuggle close to her and she buries her face in my fur to help the pain go away.

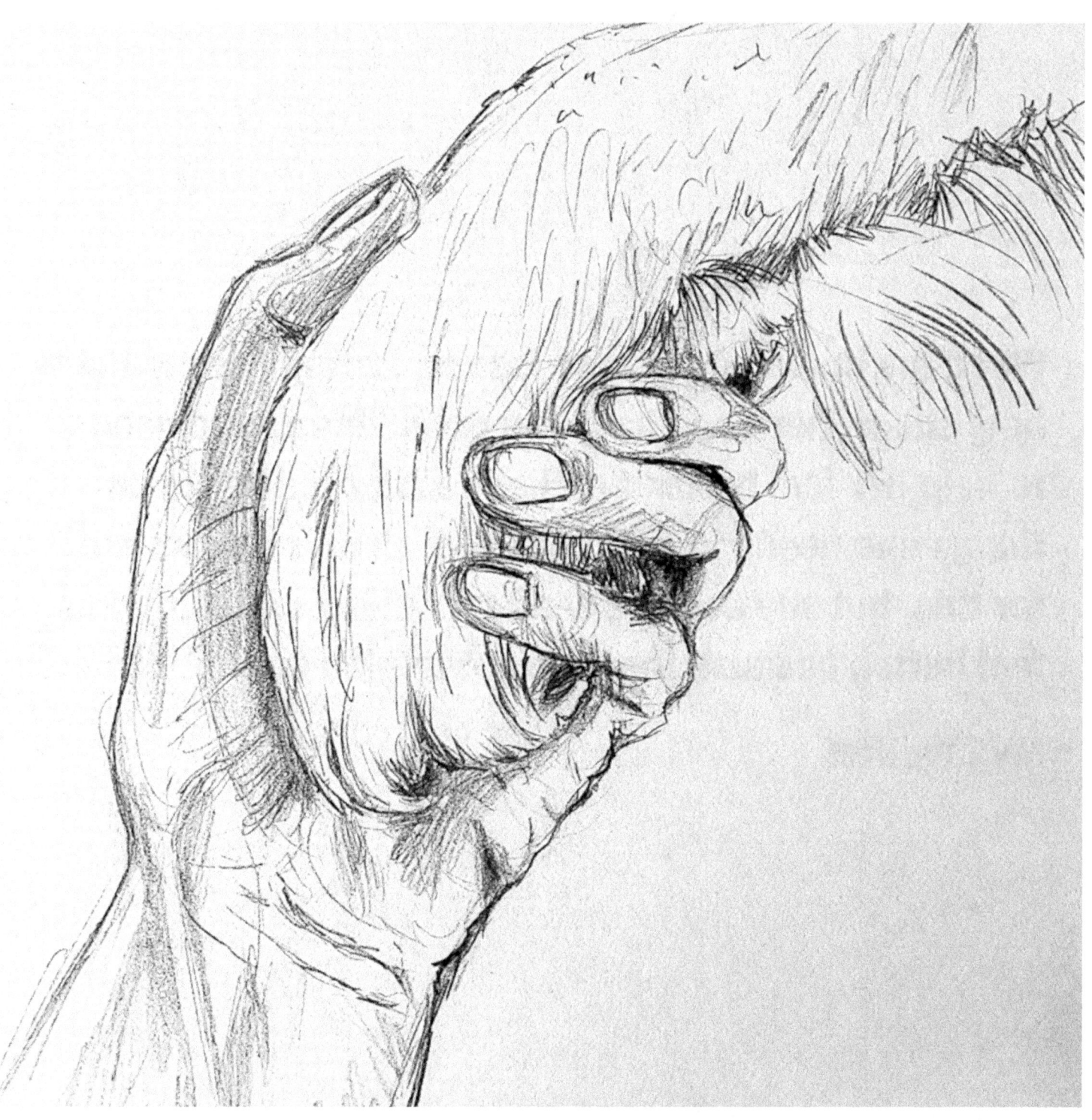

When my human has these issues, I bring her medicine bag, shoes, her book bag, and other things she needs to help her feel better. I make it easier for her to do things she needs to get done. She always thanks me for this, but she doesn't need to. I enjoy watching her feel better, because then we get to play ball!

My favorite!

PTSD means Post Traumatic Stress Disorder. It is the result of a traumatic experience or a long term trauma due to abuse. My human was abused most of her life. So, I help her calm down when she has flashbacks. Flashbacks are like dreams. They happen when you are awake and it feels like you are reliving the abuse. It's very scary to have them.

She takes me to her kung fu club. There, she instructs kids and adults how to do Ving Tsun (pronounced Wing Chun). I think she's the best instructor ever. But I am biased. She IS my human, after all!

At the end of classes I get to play with the kids sometimes. They practice hitting the ball and I get to chase it and bring it back. The kids love it. Sometimes her students have issues like my human does. And I get to help them through their panic attacks as well.

It's an important job!

My human is a great doggie teacher! She got asked to help train other service dogs. Some dogs are there to help the blind, to help others who can't move very well, and to help other people like my human who was traumatized. It's fun work to help lead the puppies to learn how to be good dogs for their humans.

I get to go everywhere where my human goes. But there are rules I have to follow. I can't pee on things, play with items on shelves, or touch things without my human's permission. I have to sit at all times, even if there are kids or other dogs I want to see and say hello to. My attention has to be on my human. It's hard at times, because I love kids and all creatures and I just really want to sniff them!

There are rules that apply to me that humans have to follow. I can't be petted without having people ask my human first. So, if you see a service dog, don't pet without asking! We are working dogs and it might be too much for our humans for those who have trauma history, coming up and just petting might set off a bad panic attack or a flashback. So keep your space and always ask before you pet a service animal.

Taking lots of walks is good for me and it is good for my human too! I get to learn to sit at the curb before we cross the street. I learn skills I get to help other dogs learn!

Practicing my skills is very important!

I love going on walks with my human. I get to sniff and learn new skills. I get to go to parks to play ball and run as fast as I can. I get to see all kinds of neat animals and plants on my walk.

It makes my nose very happy.

This is my sister Tilly. She is an older cat. She doesn't mind me too much as long as I don't stick my nose in her face. If I do stick my nose in her face, she swats me. It doesn't hurt. She just likes her personal space.

Sometimes she will snuggle with me and my human. I like snuggling with her. Her purrs are soothing.

This is my sister dog named Bella.

I love her deeply. She is a working dog, too! She helps sniff out things for her human for his work. She is a detection dog. She finds things that her human can't find on his own. Her job is very important. It helps animals in the wild be safe.

Every day I learn something new to help my human live an easier life. Because of me, she can run her kung fu club, teach other humans to train their puppies, go out and sing, and buy groceries. Things she would struggle with before I came into her life. Every day she tells me I am the best boy ever.

That I am! And every day I make my human the best she can be.

TOGETHER WE MAKE A GREAT TEAM!

~FIN~

GLOSSARY:

Trauma:
A disordered psychic or behavioral state resulting from mental or emotional stress or physical injury.

PTSD:
(Post Traumatic Stress Disorder) A psychological reaction occurring after experiencing a highly stressing event (such as wartime combat, physical violence, or a natural disaster) that is usually characterized by depression, anxiety, flashbacks, recurrent nightmares, and avoidance of reminders of the event.

Fibromyalgia:
A chronic disorder characterized by widespread pain, tenderness, and stiffness of muscles and associated connective tissue structures that is typically accompanied by fatigue, headache, and sleep disturbances.

Ball:
The best toy ever invented.

Cat:
A creature whose face I cannot stick my nose in.

Bella:
A border collie who helps detect dead things for her human. Who, as a dog, I am quite jealous of, because every dog loves the smell of dead things.

Scent Detection Dog:
A dog whose job is sniff out a particular thing, person, or creature. These dogs can be used to sniff out even cancer!

Service Dog:
A dog whose job is to help their human with a set of tasks to help make the life of their human easier. Example: guide dog, to help a blind person navigate safely in the community.

REFERENCE:
www.merriam-webster.com

Help for Humans:

USA Suicide Prevention Lifeline:

Hours: Available 24 hours.
Languages: English, Spanish.
800-273-8255

Free Text Help:

Text **HOME** to **741741** from anywhere in the United States, anytime. Crisis Text Line is here for any crisis. A live, trained Crisis Counselor receives the text and responds, all from our secure online platform. The volunteer Crisis Counselor will help you move from a hot moment to a cool moment.

Help for Dog Training:

Dog Service Training Information:

www.superstarservicedogs.net

Business 30 SW
Mount Vernon, Iowa 52314

319-775-7172
319-855-8195

Service Dogs Dos and Don'ts

1. DON'T touch a service dog without asking permission.

2. DO keep your own dog away from a working dog.

3. DON'T offer food to a service dog.

4. DO treat the owner/handler with respect.

5. DON'T assume a napping service dog is not working.

6. DO inform the handler if a service dog approaches you.

7. DON'T assume service dogs never get to 'just be dogs'.

Service dogs are working dogs. If you wish to pet a service dog, please ask permission of the handler first. If the answer is no, please be respectful.

You can make service dogs job easier by respecting the guidelines above. Service dogs may work hard, but they love helping people and you can help them by following these guidelines.

ABOUT THE AUTHOR AND ILLUSTRATOR

Ms. Stubby (Stephanie) Webb

Ms. Stubby Webb was born in 1981. She began her art journey at the age of three years old. She has illustrated other books, "Molly, the Dog with Diabetes", and "Huck & Finn, Bookstore Cats", by Kevin J Coolidge. Also illustrated, "The Littlest Cock", by Jessica Eppley.

She is an instructor at Vinton Ving Tsun Kung Fu Club in Vinton, Iowa. There she is under the Sifu (Master of Kung Fu/teacher) Instructor Program. She is earning her way to becoming a Sifu herself.

ABOUT LUCAS

Lucas was born in April 7 of 2020. He is a Border Collie. His sweet gentleness and patience is vital for his human's (Ms. Stubby) ability to succeed.

He loves to play ball, create games, and go for walks. He loves treats and snuggles. His favorite reward is being around children.

Stephanie Webb is also the illustrator of **Molly, the Dog with Diabetes**.

Molly is a true story about a dachshund-mix dog, and her journey with diabetes. Molly's story is not only a dog story, but also the story of living a happy and healthy life with diabetes.

Her story is available at From My Shelf Books & Gifts, on the Internet at www.wellsborobookstore.com, or wherever books are sold.

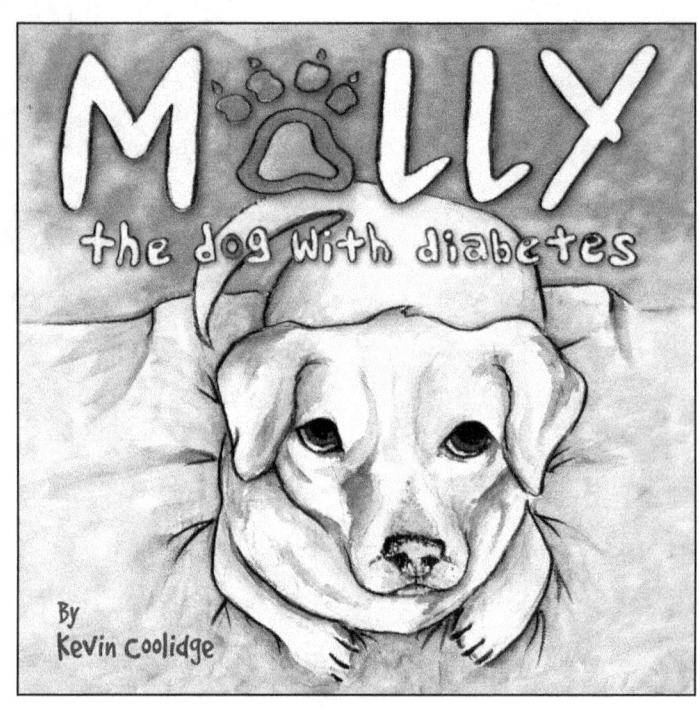

Stephanie Webb is also the illustrator of **Huck & Finn, Bookstore Cats**.

Huck & Finn are the bookstore cats at From My Shelf Books & Gifts in Wellsboro Pennsylvania. You may have seen the brothers in Bookstore Cats by Brandon Schultz. Now you can read about a day in the life of Huck & Finn at the bookstore. It's a book all their own, but they still have to share it with each other.

Huck & Finn's story is available at From My Shelf Books & Gifts, on their website at www.wellsborobookstore.com, or wherever books are sold.

Thank you to the many people who helped make my first book happen.

Kevin and Kasey, for their patience in being my first publisher.

Jackie, for helping me train my dog.

Randy, for being there to help with Lucas.

To my friends and family who believe in me; my deepest thanks!

I am a truly blessed person!

www.ingramcontent.com/pod-product-compliance
Lightning Source LLC
Chambersburg PA
CBHW060428010526
44118CB00017B/2404